In memory of my mother - D.M.
For my family - A.S.

First published in Great Britain in 1995 by
Frances Lincoln Limited, 4 Torriano Mews,
Torriano Avenue, London NW5 2RZ

British Library Cataloguing in Publication Data
available on request

ISBN 0 - 7112 - 0954 - 5

Set in Univers Light by FMT Graphics

Printed and bound in Hong Kong

1 3 5 7 9 8 6 4 2

WHAT AM I?

Debbie MacKinnon

Photographs by
Anthea Sieveking

FRANCES LINCOLN

"Nee Naw, Nee Naw!" shouts Rachel.

What is she?

Firefighter

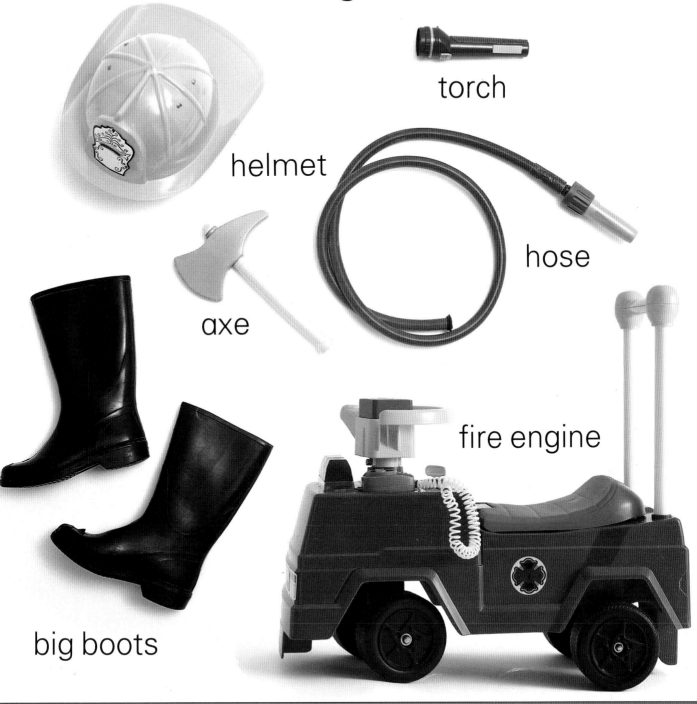

torch

helmet

axe

hose

big boots

fire engine

"The spaghetti is ready," says George.

What is he?

Cook

saucepan

spatula

frying pan

ladle

casserole

apron

whisk

"5, 4, 3, 2, 1, LIFT OFF!" shouts Mike.

What is he?

Astronaut

space suit

space glove

space boots

rockets

helmet

space station

"All together now ... 1, 2, 3!" sings Taran to Emma and Sam.

What are they?

Musicians

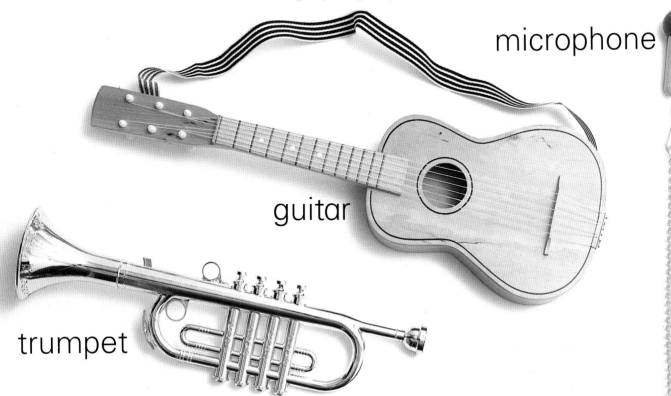

microphone

guitar

trumpet

cassette player

tambourine

"Load up!" Lucy tells William.

What is she?

Farmer

straw hat

rake

shovel

dungarees

straw

trailer

tractor

"Where does it hurt?" asks Lara.

What is she?

Doctor

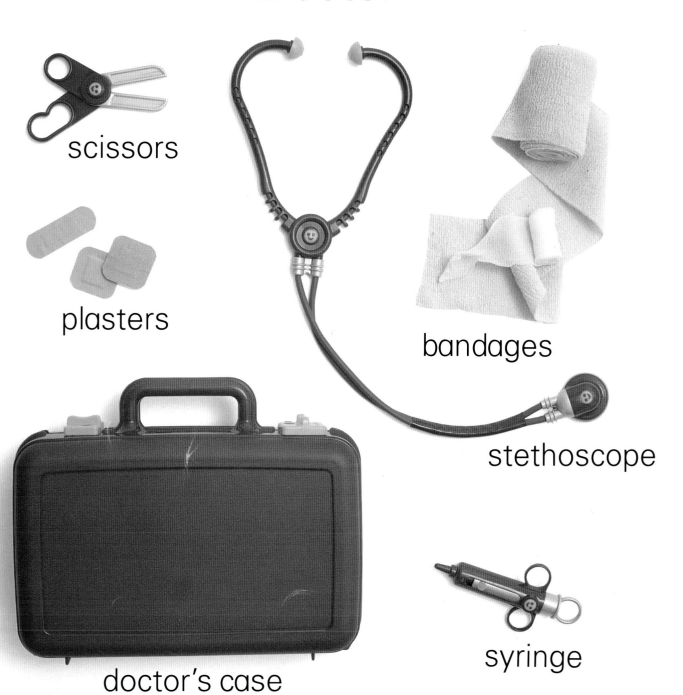

scissors

plasters

bandages

stethoscope

doctor's case

syringe

"The circus is coming!" calls Tom.

What is he?

Clown

braces

face paints

wig

nose

bow-tie

juggling balls

trousers

silly shoes

Parents

Mummy's hat

necklaces

Daddy's waistcoat

handbag

baby

buggy

Mummy's shoes

Daddy's shoes